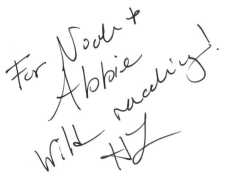

Mary's Wild Winter Feast

Hannah Lindoff

Illustrated by Nobu Koch and Clarissa Rizal

University of Alaska Press

Fairbanks

University of Alaska Press
P.O. Box 756240
Fairbanks, AK 99775-6240

Library of Congress Cataloging-in-Publication Data
Lindoff, Hannah.
  Mary's wild winter feast / by Hannah Lindoff ; images by Nobu Koch and Clarissa Rizal.
    pages cm
  Summary: When rain spoils her plans for sledding, Mary wishes that Alaska were not
her homeland, but her father shows her, through jars of salmon, seaweed, berries, and
more in their pantry, just how special a place it is.
  ISBN 978-1-60223-232-7 (pbk. : alk. paper)
  1. Alaska—Juvenile fiction. [1. Alaska—Fiction. 2. Fathers and daughters—Fiction.]
I. Koch, Nobu, illustrator. II. Rizal, Clarissa, illustrator.
II. Title.
  PZ7.L65914Mar 2014
  [E]--dc23
                        2013049805

Cover design by Dixon Jones

This publication was printed on acid-free paper that meets the minimum requirements for
ANSI / NISO Z39.48–1992 (R2002) (Permanence of Paper for Printed Library Materials).

Production Date: April 24, 2014
Plant & Location: Printed by Everbest Printing (Guangzhou, China), Co. Ltd
Job / Batch #41556-0 / 702077

Introduction

Mary's Wild Winter Feast celebrates two strong relationships: one between an Alaska family and the bountiful land and water of Southeast Alaska, and the second between a father and his daughter.

The family in this story reflects my own family. My husband is Alaska Native, both Tlingit and Haida, and I have been adopted into a Tlingit clan. Together, our family carries on many Southeast Native traditions. Our favorites bring us closer to the land and sea on harvesting adventures. We share our adventures with others from all kinds of families.

I asked Tlingit artist Clarissa Rizal to create collages for the magnificent illustrations painted by lifelong Juneauite Nobu Koch. Clarissa also loves gathering indigenous foods, and her collages invoke the beautiful bond between the Tlingit people and their homeland. What an honor to see this amazing artwork become part of my book!

Enjoy!

Hannah

To my Mari, and her daddy.

Bump, bump, bump!

Mary stretched out her legs and slid down the stairs one at a time. She closed her eyes and imagined herself on a sled. But it didn't work. Bumping down the stairs felt nothing like sledding.

Mary looked out the window. Wind blew rain sideways into the panes with a splat! Cold water trickled down the glass. The snow had melted, taking with it Mary's hope of sledding today. A cold winter rainstorm poured on Juneau, Alaska.

"It's so horrible outside, Daddy!" Mary groaned. She traced a raindrop's path down the windowpane. "Why do we live here?"

Daddy looked up from his newspaper. "How can you ask that, Silly Bear? This is our homeland. I love it here."

Mary looked at the wet sledding hill outside. Her breath fogged the cold windowpane. Mud and gravel from the street flecked the base of the hill. Yesterday Mary and her cousins had packed snow into a jump at the base of the hill. Now the jump sat like a sad, white bump on the green and brown slope. It, too, slowly melted under the cold rain.

"Daddy, why did we get this homeland? Why aren't we from somewhere more fun?" Mary frowned.

"Where in the world could be more fun than here?" asked Daddy. "Come with me, Mary. I want to show you something."

Mary followed him into the kitchen. He opened the door to the pantry.

Jars of food filled the tiny room. There were small jars, tall jars, and round, fat jars. Jars stacked on jars sat on the shelves. Jars full of different foods even lined the floor!

Salmon

Daddy took a jar off the middle shelf and showed it to Mary. On one side of the jar Mary saw pink. On the other side silver scales pressed against the glass.

"Do you know what this is, Little Bear?" he asked Mary.

"It's salmon, Daddy," said Mary.

"Yes, it is salmon. I got this salmon for you and Mama last summer. Remember, when the fireweed blooms pink and purple, it's time to go fishing!

"We left very early in the morning. Uncle Boots took his boat. I took my boat. We went out with the tide, out into the ocean. We passed three wild islands where no people live. We kept the boat close to the last island and drove near the shore until we found the big river.

"When you are older, Mary, you can ride in my boat. Your eyes will find the river."

"And find the salmon?" Mary asked.

"Yes," said Daddy. "Finding the salmon is the most important part. Then the tide changed. As the waves came in they pushed the fish toward the river. We saw the fish sliding out of the ocean into the river. If we didn't catch them right away, we would have to wait for the next tide!"

"How did you catch them?" asked Mary.

"We took a long net and put it in the water. Then I drove my boat away, and the net stretched between our boats. The fish kept coming—bang! Into the net!

"I love pulling fish out of my net. You will like that part too, Mary. It's like opening one hundred birthday presents. You can hold each fish in your hand and see how firm and tasty it looks. In just one set we pulled out enough for our families and the elders too!"

"I do like birthday presents," said Mary. "I got a sled for my birthday, but now I can't use it."

Daddy raised his eyebrows and continued. "You, Mama, and I ate fresh salmon that night! Then we cut up what we couldn't eat and put it in jars. We sent some to Great-Grandpa so he could have salmon sandwiches all winter."

"Mmm," said Mary, brightening. "That sounds good. Let's have salmon sandwiches, Daddy!"

"Not yet, Mare Bear," he replied. "What do you think about your homeland now?"

Mary's smile disappeared. "Salmon come from my home*water*s," she replied stubbornly.

Daddy laughed. "I have more jars to show you."

Deer

Daddy held up another jar. "Do you know what this is?" Red-brown chunks of meat filled the jar.

"It's deer."

"Yes! It's deer. I got this deer for us last fall. Uncle Boots and I left before daylight. We took my boat over to the bay. What a cold boat ride! The wind blew hard, but my wool coat kept me warm.

"When we got to the island we pulled the boat out of the water. We tugged it right up onto the beach. Then

we ate the cookies you and Mama made. Those kept me warm too.

"As the sun rose we started up the mountain. It was so steep that sometimes we had to pull ourselves up on tree branches. You climb like a monkey, Mary. When you are bigger, will you lead the way for us?"

"I will! When I lead the way I hold the branches so they don't swing back and hit you."

"That's exactly what we need! On this hunt we had to be very careful. A wrong turn could have taken us to a rock wall where we would have been stuck!

"In three hours we were so high up on the mountain we no longer saw trees. Trees can't grow that high up. Deer country is very beautiful. Deer come there to eat small plants. They drink from many tiny lakes. Flowers grow everywhere."

"I want to go to deer country, Daddy!" said Mary.

"You will come with me soon, Mary," he replied. "You will love exploring a new part of your homeland."

"Yeah, I think I need to see the top of this homeland before I can decide if I like it," said Mary.

"Okay," Daddy agreed. "But you must get a little bigger and a little better at staying quiet! You have to be quiet when you are looking for deer.

"I spotted a buck across the meadow, so I lay down on my belly to hide. Then I crawled through the bushes to take aim. As I crawled along I almost crawled right into another deer!

"Uncle and I both came home happy, with deer for our families. We jarred this up to keep the tender meat for later.

"And do you remember making this one?" Daddy held up a similar warm-brown jar.

"My deer stew! Yes, I remember it!" said Mary. "You cooked the meat and Mama and I filled the jars. We made layers: first broth, then meat, then carrots, potatoes, and onions, then meat again. That was fun."

"I always have fun cooking with you and Mama," said Daddy. "You did a great job on the stew. It's the perfect meal; all we have to do is heat it up."

Mary put the jar to her lips. "Let's heat one up now!"

"Not now, Goofy Bear. I want to show you something else," said Daddy.

Dried Seaweed

"Do you know what this is?" Daddy held up a large jar. Black flecks just covered the bottom of the jar. The rest stood empty.

"Black seaweed!" Mary cried.

"That's right! You remember this seaweed, Baby Bear; you ate most of it! We got it together last spring. We took a small plane over to Hoonah for the weekend."

"It was such a small plane that I got to sit right next to the pilot!" said Mary.

"You flew co-pilot! We brought sleeping bags and
pillows so we could sleep on Captain Seahawk's big
fishing boat. At eleven at night the tide was right for the
boat to leave. You were sleepy by then. We walked down
to the docks and I lifted you onto the fishing boat deck."

"Walking on the deck was hard at first," said Mary.

"Captain Seahawk and his wife, Honey, let you and
Mama and the baby sleep in the stateroom at the front of
the boat."

"We slept all together in one bunk. It was squashy, but the sound of the engine and the rocking put us right to sleep. Where did you sleep, Daddy?"

"Captain Seahawk and I were having too much fun to sleep. The moon shone bright and full over our heads, so we decided to surprise you and Mama. Do you remember what you saw on the deck when you woke up in the morning?"

"Halibut! Three fat halibut on a bed of ice on the deck."

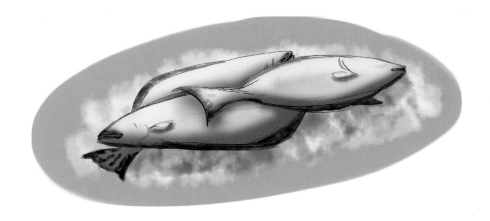

"That's right. We gave Honey the wheel and went out jigging in the skiff by the light of the moon. We landed three plump halibut.

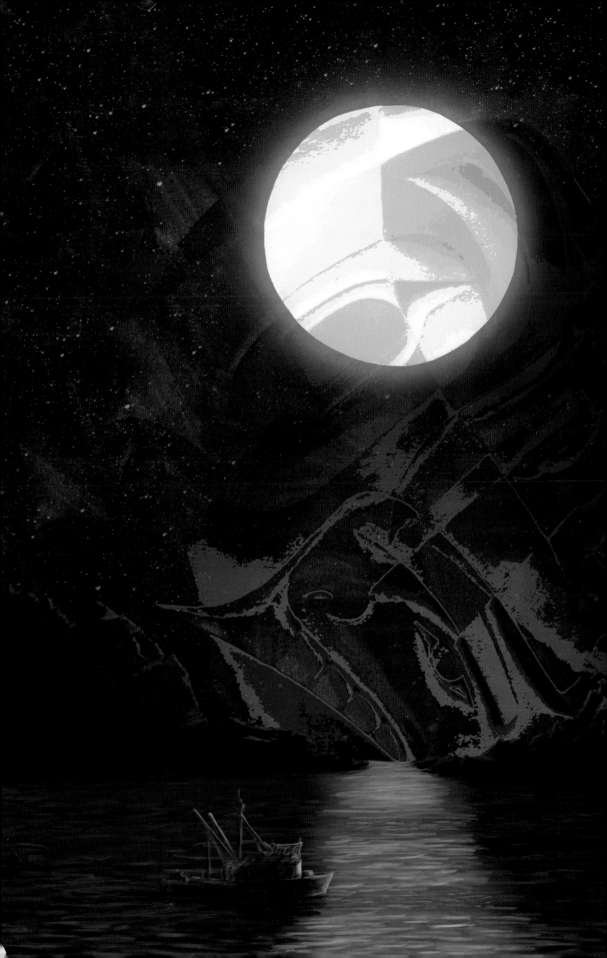

"The big boat traveled far while you and Mama and the baby slept. In the morning we anchored the boat and loaded everyone into the skiff. We drove the skiff up to the gravel beach on an island.

"Gravel covered one side of the island. A few trees grew near the edges on high ground. The other side is normally under water but it was low tide. The big rocks on the sea floor lay open to the fresh spring air. It was the lowest tide of the year, which is perfect for harvesting seaweed!

"You and I walked carefully over the rocks to the other side of the island. I almost slipped a few times on the wet red seaweed," said Daddy.

"I slipped on the seaweed too, but you caught me!" Mary said.

"Of course I did, Clumsy Bear," said Daddy. "At the far beach we faced the big, wide ocean and some far-off mountains still white with snow. There we found the black seaweed. We pulled it up off the rocks by the handful. First one, then two, and in no time at all, we filled the bucket!

"Then we took out butter knives and you helped me look for gumboots."

"Once Honey showed me what they look like, they were easy to find," said Mary. "They stick to rocks. Their black shells hide in the dark parts of the tide pools. I scanned my eyes across the rocks in rows. That way I found all the gumboots hiding there."

"Yes," said Daddy. "You found so many that my arms got sore from prying them off the rocks with my knife. We had to sit down on the gravel beach and rest."

"And roast some marshmallows," said Mary with a smile.

"On the boat ride home we passed the seagull nesting grounds and sea lion rocks. Honey taught you songs while Captain Seahawk drove the boat. It felt nice to ride in the warm boat with our friends after reaching into the cold ocean water all morning."

"That was a fun trip, Daddy!" Mary said.

Daddy continued, "At home we took the closet door off its hinges and put it outside. We spread the seaweed out on the door and let it dry in the sun. Then I ground up the seaweed into these chunks. And wouldn't you know it, Uncle Boots stopped by to help! He says dried black seaweed tastes better than popcorn."

"Yes! It is better!" cried Mary. "Why don't I just finish what's left in the jar so we can wash it out for next year?"

"Hungry Bear! I'm not done!" Daddy smiled.

Blueberries

Daddy held up two purple jars. "What's in these jars?"

"Blueberries, of course!" said Mary. She kept the big jar with the last of the seaweed in her arms.

"These are jarred blueberries and here is your auntie's blueberry jam," said Daddy. "Blueberries are fun to pick because we can go together as a family. You, Mama, the baby, and I all love blueberries!

"We got these berries on a hot summer day. We drove to our secret blueberry spot where no one else picks.

The berries hung on the bushes, round and dark. They covered the hillside."

"I picked so many berries my fingers turned blue!" Mary remembered.

"You ate so many berries your lips turned blue too," said Daddy.

"As we headed home with full berry buckets, we saw the bushes moving. Was there another family picking our berries? Did they follow us to our secret spot?

"No! Through the bushes we saw a mama bear and two cubs! We did not want to meet the bears. We walked away quickly, back up the hill."

"Then you told me to yell," said Mary. "So I *yelled*."

"Yes, you are good at making noise," said Daddy. "The noise told the bears where we stood. The bear family heard us and moved away. They didn't want to

meet us either. We have to remember, this isn't just our homeland."

"That's okay," said Mary, "I like bears. I can share with them."

Daddy smiled. "That night Mama made a blueberry pie and we invited Auntie for dessert. Then we jarred up the rest of the berries so we could eat them later on ice cream.

"Auntie knows that you like jam on toast so she made blueberry jam for you!"

"I do like jam on toast, Daddy, but I think I'd rather have ice cream today," said Mary.

"Mmm, so would I, Sweetie Bear, but not now," he replied. "I have more jars to show you."

Smoked Salmon

Daddy held up a half-pint jar filled with red strips. "Do you know what this is?"

"It's salmon again!"

"Not just salmon, Little Bear, it's smoked sockeye! The best salmon in the world! It tastes sweet, but not too sweet. It tastes salty, but not too salty. It's rich and smoky and perfect!

"Last fall I went fishing with Uncle Boots. We wanted to make one more salmon harvest for the season. We started my boat in the darkness before the sun rose. Fallen leaves turned the air musty. I felt autumn in the cool weather. Luckily, it didn't take long to get to the creek.

"This time we cast-netted. I rolled up the net, then I threw it where I saw a salmon.

Splash! It hit a rock!

I rolled it up and threw it again.

Splash! I pulled the net in but it was empty.

Splash! I caught a stick.

At last I got the hang of it. Splash! I got a salmon!
After that, almost every splash brought me a fish."

"When you brought it home, I helped you smoke it," said Mary proudly.

"Yes, I love having a good helper like you," said Daddy.

"We lit a fire in the smokehouse and hung the salmon on the racks. The smoke came up and lent its flavor to the fish."

"Then you cut up the salmon and I put it in the jars," Mary remembered.

"Yes," Daddy said. "We put oil in the jars to make the sockeye soft and good for eating with crackers."

"Mmm, Daddy, I found the crackers!" said Mary. She pointed at a high shelf.

"But Mary Beary, we haven't looked at the soap berries, fish eggs, puff mushrooms, pickled gumboots, or the beach asparagus yet," said Daddy with a twinkle in his eye.

"Grandma sent these over from Hoonah. Do you know why Grandma is the best at getting gumboots?"

"Why?" asked Mary.

"Because she's so stubborn she can pry them off the rock with just a look!"

"A look like this, Daddy?" asked Mary. She scrunched up her nose and narrowed her eyes.

"Yes, just like that, Scary Bear!"

"But my look didn't work. I was trying to pry the lid off the smoked sockeye so we could have it for lunch!"

"Silly Bear!" laughed Daddy. He took a jar of smoked salmon off the shelf and handed it to Mary. He grabbed the deer stew, the gumboots, and the jarred blueberries too. "Let's have a feast!"

Mary took her jars and sat at the table. "You know what, Daddy?"

"What, Mare Bear?"

"I don't want a different homeland. This is a pretty good place to live."